The Wild World of Animals

Earthworms

Underground Burrowers

by Adele D. Richardson

Consultant:
Dennis Linden
U.S. Department of Agriculture
Agricultural Research Service

Bridgestone Books
an imprint of Capstone Press
Mankato, Minnesota

Bridgestone Books are published by Capstone Press
151 Good Counsel Drive, P.O. Box 669, Mankato, Minnesota 56002
http://www.capstone-press.com

Library of Congress Cataloging-in-Publication Data
Richardson, Adele, 1966–
   Earthworms: Underground burrowers/by Adele D. Richardson.
   p. cm.—(The wild world of animals)
   Includes bibliographical references (p. 24) and index.
   ISBN 0-7368-0826-4
   1. Earthworms—Juvenile literature. [1. Earthworms.] I. Title. II. Series.
QL391.A6 R53 2001
592'.64—dc21

                                                                    00-010282

Summary: A simple introduction to earthworms describing their physical characteristics, habitat, young, food, enemies, and relationship to people.

Editorial Credits
Sarah Lynn Schuette, editor; Karen Risch, product planning editor; Linda Clavel, designer
   and illustrator; Kimberly Danger and Heidi Schoof, photo researchers

Photo Credits
Bill Beatty, 16
Dwight R. Kuhn, 4, 8, 10, 12, 14, 20
GeoIMAGERY/Robert Winslow, 18
Linda Clavel, 1
Unicorn Stock Photos/Tom Edwards, 6
Visuals Unlimited/Steve Maslowski, cover

1 2 3 4 5 6 06 05 04 03 02 01

Table of Contents

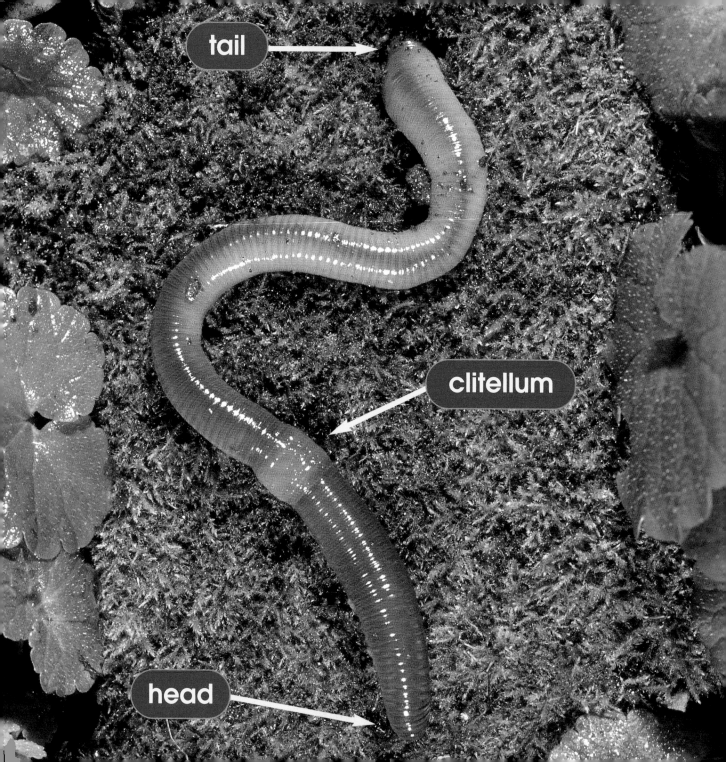

Earthworms

Earthworms have long, thin bodies covered by moist skin. They have small hairs called chaetae all over their bodies. A clitellum wraps around the middle of the body. Both ends of earthworms are pointed. An earthworm's head often looks like its tail.

Earthworms Are Invertebrates

Earthworms are invertebrates. They do not have backbones. Earthworms also are annelids. Annelids have long, soft bodies made up of many ring-shaped segments.

segment
a part or section of something

FUN FACTS

Earthworms breathe
through their skin.

Underground Burrowers

Earthworms often crawl in warm, wet soil. Some earthworms live close to the surface of the soil. Others dig deep burrows in the ground. Earthworms hide from enemies under rocks, logs, or rotting leaves.

burrow

a hole or tunnel in the ground where an animal lives

FUN FACTS

Earthworms have five hearts. Each heart pumps blood to a different part of its body.

What Do Earthworms Eat?

Earthworms eat rotting plants and vegetables. They also eat the remains of animals. Earthworms swallow soil and small rocks with their food. The soil and rocks help earthworms grind up food inside their body.

earthworm cocoon

Earthworm Eggs

Earthworms have both male and female body parts. Earthworms join their clitellums to mate during spring and summer. Adult earthworms wrap eggs inside a cocoon on the ground. Some eggs take weeks or months to hatch.

mate
to join together to produce young

earthworm hatching

Young Earthworms

Adult earthworms do not take care of their young. Young earthworms are smaller than adult earthworms. But they grow quickly. A young earthworm grows to be an adult in about 90 days. Adult earthworms do not live long. Many die after one week in the wild.

Earthworm Enemies

Earthworms have many enemies. Birds, frogs, and snakes eat earthworms. Some people use earthworms for fishing bait. Chaetae help earthworms protect themselves from enemies. Earthworms grab on to the sides of their burrows with these hairs.

protect
to guard or to keep something from harm

FUN FACTS

Earthworms are many sizes. Some earthworms are as small as 1 inch (2.5 centimeters) long. The giant African earthworm is the largest earthworm in the world. It can grow to be 22 feet (7 meters) long.

Regeneration

Earthworms can regenerate. An enemy sometimes breaks an earthworm's body apart. Earthworms can sometimes grow a new tail or head. They often die when they try to grow a new head. Earthworms cannot eat without their heads.

regenerate
to grow again

Fertilizing the Soil

Earthworm castings help the soil in gardens and fields stay rich and healthy. Some people have worm bins. They put earthworms and rotting food inside these bins. Earthworms eat the food and make castings. People then use the castings to fertilize their gardens.

castings
earthworm waste

Hands On: Loose Soil

Farmers and gardeners like earthworms because they loosen and fertilize soil. Loose soil helps plants grow. This activity will show you the difference between hard soil and loose soil.

What You Need

Plastic shovel
Small area of soil outside
Stick
Small pieces of tape

What You Do

1. Use the shovel to dig up a small area of soil. The area should be about 6 inches (15 centimeters) square. Do not remove the soil. Just loosen it up in the ground.
2. Pick up the stick. Gently push the stick in the soil you did not touch with the shovel. Mark how far the stick goes into the ground with a piece of tape.
3. Push the stick into the loosened soil using the same force as before. Mark how far this stick went into the ground. Compare the two tape marks.

The stick goes much farther into the loose dirt. In the same way, water and air will get to a plant's roots easier in loose soil. Water and air help plants grow. Earthworms loosen the soil when they dig burrows.

Words to Know

annelids (AN-uh-lids)—a group of animals that are long invertebrates and have segmented bodies

chaetae (KEE-tee)—small hairs; chaetae help protect earthworms from their enemies.

clitellum (cli-TEL-um)—a band around the middle of an earthworm; earthworms join their clitellums to mate.

cocoon (kuh-KOON)—a protective covering made of silky threads

fertilize (FUR-tuh-lize)—to make soil rich and healthy; earthworms help to fertilize the ground.

invertebrate (in-VUR-tuh-brit)—an animal without a backbone

regenerate (re-JEN-uh-rayt)—to grow again

Read More

Himmelman, John. *An Earthworm's Life.* Nature Upclose. New York: Children's Press, 2000.

Holmes, Kevin J. *Earthworms.* Animals. Mankato, Minn.: Bridgestone Books, 1998.

Internet Sites

Adventures of Herman
http://www.urbanext.uiuc.edu/worms/index.html
Worm Watch Canada-Cool Stuff
http://www.cciw.ca/ecowatch/wormwatch/english/cool/cool.htm#facts
Yucky Worm World
http://www.yucky.com/worm

Index